STEAM UP! TRACTION ENGINES ON PARADE

DAVID REED

AMBERLEY

To my brother Roger,
Diane, Emma and Peter

First published 2024

Amberley Publishing
The Hill, Stroud
Gloucestershire, GL5 4EP

www.amberley-books.com

Copyright © David Reed, 2024

The right of David Reed to be identified as
the Author of this work has been asserted in
accordance with the Copyrights, Designs and
Patents Act 1988.

ISBN 978 1 3981 1803 4 (print)
ISBN 978 1 3981 1804 1 (ebook)

British Library Cataloguing in Publication Data.
A catalogue record for this book is available from
the British Library.

Origination by Amberley Publishing.
Printed in the UK.

Introduction

My interest in traction engines was encouraged by my parents, Margaret and Jimmy Reed, from a very early age. With them I attended rallies organised by the Andover & District Model Engineering Society at Finkley Manor Farm, Andover. Although we visited rallies when I was quite young, the first programme I have for an Andover traction engine rally is their fifteenth, dated 9 and 10 September 1967, when I was sixteen. This was the society's first two-day rally, and my first traction engine photographs date back to this event. I started taking traction engine images after photographing the end of steam locomotives on the Waterloo to Bournemouth railway line.

To photograph the last of the steam trains I borrowed my mother's old Purma Plus camera; these pictures are chronicled in my first book, *Steam Railways: Final Operations on the Southern Region and the Early Preservation Years*. My early colour slides of traction engines were taken with the same Purma Plus camera on Kodak Ektachrome 127 roll film, which had to be taken to the chemist to be sent off for developing. The Purma camera had a fixed f6.3 lens aperture and three shutter speeds, 1/25, 1/150 and 1/500. After starting work in the 1970s I graduated to a basic Zenith 35 mm single-lens reflex camera, which gave me more flexibility.

By 1969 the Andover event had become known as a Steam & Vintage Rally. This indicated a desire to broaden the range of interest to include cars, tractors and other vehicles and attract the general public rather than just steam enthusiasts. In 1971 I attended the Hungerford Olde Tyme Fayre and Steam Engine Rally and in 1972 the Basingstoke Steam & Transport Festival. A number of Fairground Organ Festivals at the Montague Motor Museum, now the National Motor Museum, Beaulieu, were also visited around this time, which more narrowly featured the colourful showmen's engines and fairground organs. It wasn't until some years later that I attended my first Great Working of Steam Engines at Stourpaine Bushes organised by the Dorset Steam & Historic Vehicle Club. This went on to become the Great Dorset Steam Fair, which is now held on the enormous site at Tarrant Hinton, near Blandford Forum, Dorset.

For readers less familiar with traction engines, here follows a few words about the various types. A general-purpose traction engine is probably what most people imagine, that is an engine that can be used for anything, mainly in an agricultural setting. They brought mechanisation to the farm such as driving a threshing machine or circular saw bench and moving produce around much as a diesel farm tractor does now.

Portable engines, which needed to be towed from job to job either by a traction engine or horses, could also be used for farm work. Prior to threshing machines, work such as threshing or thrashing would have been backbreaking labour, done by hand by beating the corn on the threshing floor of a barn. Sawing would have been done by a pair of men, one probably standing in a saw pit while they pushed and pulled a double-ended saw between them.

Steam ploughing engines operate by pulling a double-ended plough back and forth between a pair of engines on either side of a field. Multiple furrows could be quickly made compared with one furrow at a time by a man with a horse.

A steamroller does what the name says, being used before the days of tarmacadam to roll the road to consolidate stones and gravel into the surface. Many rollers had a scarifier fitted at the rear, comprising a bracket fitted with downward-facing prongs that would be lowered to break up the old road surface. Sometimes rollers would haul tar spreaders that would heat the tar and spread it ready to accept the surface gravel similarly to the winter-proofing of modern roads with tar and chippings.

A steam tractor is a small- to medium-sized engine designed to haul loads over some distance like a motor van or small lorry does. A road locomotive is a larger engine designed for heavy haulage in much the same way as a modern articulated lorry. Road locomotives usually have additional water tanks underneath and could be seen hauling heavy loads such as boilers from steelworks to factories, effectively moving the products of the industrial age around the country.

There were fairground showman's variants of both steam tractors and road locomotives, which featured brightly polished brass decorations and other embellishments. Most importantly, they carried a dynamo on a bracket in front of the chimney, driven by a belt from the flywheel, to generate power for lighting the rides and later powering the electrically driven rides. On twisted brass supports they would carry a full-length canopy, on which the showman would advertise his latest ride.

On the fairgrounds, gallopers, otherwise known as roundabouts or carousels, appeared in Victorian years and were originally powered by a steam engine in the centre of the ride. The drive was transmitted by a shaft to an overhead gear wheel with cogs to operate the 'galloping' cranks from which the horses were suspended. Switchback rides, which consisted of wheeled cars on an undulating track with two hills and two dips, were also powered by their own steam centre engine. Gentle as they seem to us now, these were the white-knuckle rides of their time.

The gigantic scenic railway rides came after the steam switchbacks. They were a modernised, larger and grander version of the switchback ride, but with the cars individually powered by their own electric motors. Because they did not need a steam centre engine, the inside of the machine was devoted to elaborate scenery and waterfalls, hence the 'scenic' name. The starting of these rides required a lot of electric power to get the heavy cars on the move and gave rise to development of special scenic showman's engines, which had an additional exciter dynamo mounted behind the chimney to help control the electric power to start the cars. They also had a crane mounted on the coal bunker to help move the weighty cars between road trailers and the ride. The scenic railways were very large and heavy machines needing large teams of men to erect and operate. As with all rides the showmen vied with each other to be bigger and grander than their competitors.

Gallopers, switchbacks and scenic railways, together with the other various riding machines, usually had a mechanical organ to provide musical accompaniment and attract the punters. In the era before radio and television many people, especially in country villages, would not have seen or heard exciting entertainment like this. Their musical experience may not have gone beyond a parlour piano or a church band.

I made very few notes at the time I took the pictures so have had to rely on my memory, rally programmes, numerous magazines and books for information. A few of the pictures were taken by my late father, Jimmy Reed, but the rest of the photographs were taken by me, and none have been previously published.

I would like to thank my wife, Margaret, for her support during the compilation of this book and for checking my manuscript. I also thank Amberley for publishing this, the fourth book of my photographs.

Thanks are also due to the owners and operating crew of the engines and other equipment, who have saved them and continue to present them to the public and give so much enjoyment. Through these pictures I hope you will enjoy visiting some vintage steam rallies over the years.

Burrell 5-ton tractor No. 3846 *Pous Nouk Nouk* of 1920 was owned at this time by Mrs W. H. McAlpine. It is seen in a rather attractive blue livery at the Andover Rally held in September 1967.

Burrell showman's road loco No. 3295 *Princess Royal* is seen with its canopy lights illuminated at the 1967 Andover Rally. It was built in 1911 as a road haulage loco and converted to showman's specification in 1921. It is now known by the name *Erins Pride Leads the Way*.

With a Royal Navy theme at Andover in 1967 is Super Sentinel steam waggon DX9048 *HMS Sultan*. It was built in 1930 and converted to pneumatic tyres in 1933. It was bought for preservation in 1957 and loaned to the HMS Sultan Royal Navy base at Gosport. In 1970 it was bought by the Royal Navy and continues to be run by Navy volunteers.

Exhibits parade into the ring at Andover in September 1967. Maclaren traction engine No. 1160 *The Favourite* of 1912 is followed by Foden 6-ton steam wagon No. 13138 *London Pride* of 1928 and another Foden lorry, No. 11538 *The Dorset Rambler* of 1922.

Resplendent in a new coat of paint, Foden steam wagon No. 13138 *London Pride* takes part in the Grand Parade at the 1967 Andover rally. The wagon was built for Fuller's Brewery of Chiswick in 1928 and owned at this time by T. T. Boughton of Amersham.

Burrell No. 3192 *St Bernard* was built in 1910 as a Gold Medal crane tractor for the War Department. Around 1920 when in the ownership of J. H. Herbert, amusement caterer of Dorchester, it was converted to showman's specification as seen here. It was bought for preservation by the Gilbey family and has been owned by them ever since.

Burrell Gold Medal Tractor No. 3815 *Sun Set No 2*, built in 1919 and owned from 1952 by Lieutenant Commander J. M. Baldock RN, is seen driven by him at Andover in 1967. My late mother, Margaret, is steering the engine in the Ladies Invitation Steering Competition, a feature of the Andover rallies for some years. My mother also served in the Royal Navy as a Wren during the Second World War, and she was very impressed by Commander Baldock's starched white overalls! He was already well known for his Hollycombe steam and fairground collection and opened the 1967 Andover rally.

The author's mother is seen again steering *Sun Set No 2*. She won the Ladies Invitation Steering Competition and, together with my father, was invited to the Annual Dinner of the Andover & District Model Engineering Society. She was presented with a very nice pen stand, incorporating a traction engine medallion, which I still have.

Burrell steam tractor No. 3815 *Sun Set No 2* is seen at rest and being admired during a quieter moment at Andover in 1967.

Edward Hine's 1918 Fowler Tiger showman's tractor No. 14412, named *Tiger*, poses at Andover in 1967. My mother also steered *Tiger* in the Ladies Steering Competition when it was previously owned by James Harris of Poole, but didn't win that time! A picture of *Tiger* being given a lift to a rally on an elderly green Foden lorry featured on the cover of the August 1962 *Meccano Magazine*.

Also at Andover in 1967 is Wallis & Steevens 8-ton agricultural engine No. 7115 *Boxer's Beauty*, not far from its birthplace at the North Hants Ironworks, Station Hill, Basingstoke.

Two of Edward Hine's superb engines and one of his organs are being enjoyed by an enthusiastic audience at Andover in 1967. His 89-key Gavioli Black Forest Continental fair organ can be seen on the left together with his Fowler showman's tractor *Tiger* and his immaculate and very well-known Burrell Scenic showman's engine No. 3938 *Quo Vadis*.

A Limonaire 87-key fairground organ is portrayed at Andover in September 1967. Owned since 1965 by Edward Hines of Shaftsbury, it had previously been travelled in a set of gallopers. It is believed to have been built in the early 1900s, or as the 1967 rally programme said, 'about 50 years ago'.

Burrell Scenic showman's loco No. 3887 *Prince of Wales*, proclaiming itself 'Pride of the West', is looking resplendent in the ownership of James & Crockerell of Durrington, Wiltshire. It was purchased in 1956 and is pictured here at the Andover rally in September 1968.

Fowler roller No. 18637, supplied new in 1930 to Clevedon Urban District Council, poses at Andover in 1968. It has always been known as *The Roller with No Name*. According to the programme, it was first purchased for preservation in 1963 and in 1965 was bought by a group based in Herriard, near Basingstoke.

Aveling & Porter Type E road roller No. 10997 *The Enborne Queen* is seen here at Andover in 1968. It was built in 1924 and bought for preservation in 1966. Note the maroon-coloured flywheel and front roll forks typical of this manufacturer. Parked behind are the living van for the roller crew and the water dandy, a cart carrying a spare water supply.

At the time of this photograph taken at Andover in 1968, Burrell Special Scenic showman's engine No. 4000 *Ex Mayor* had just been bought by William McAlpine. The engine was delivered new to G. T. Tuby in 1925. In 1946 it was preserved by its driver and underwent extensive restoration, being repainted in maroon as seen here. William McAlpine later restored its 'Tuby Blue' livery.

Here is Burrell showman's engine No. 3443 *Lord Nelson* at Andover in 1968 in the ownership of Lord Montague of Beaulieu. It was delivered new to Anderton & Rowland in February 1913 and in 1940 passed into the hands of John Cole of Yate, Bristol. It was preserved in 1959, still fitted with its massive original 275-amp Mather & Platt dynamo.

Taskers of Andover was a well-known builder of steam tractors and rollers. Taken in 1968, this picture shows Tasker showman's tractor No. 1822 *Little Jim II*, built in 1920 as a steam tractor. It was acquired by Sam Smart of Warminster, who converted it to showman's specification. Sold in 1939, it became derelict and was bought for preservation in the mid-1960s by Chris Barber.

This instrument, named *Shaharazad*, was built in 1894 by Louis Hooguy as a barrel organ. In 1906 it was converted at Hooguy's works to play by concertina punched card. I still have the 33 rpm LP record of this organ on the Marble Arch label, which my father bought at this rally.

Shaharazad is pictured again at Andover in 1968 with power being supplied by Chris Barber's Tasker *Little Jim II*. At this time *Shaharazad* was owned by Brian Oram of St Mary Bourne, Hampshire, and mounted in a Ford Thames Trader lorry. During the First World War the organ was laid up in a barn and was retired from fairground use after the Second World War.

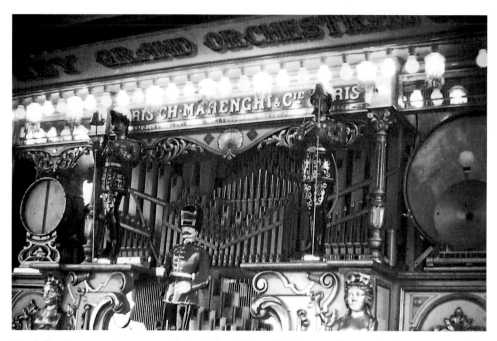

The following two pictures are of the 89-key Marenghi fairground organ built new in 1903 for Connolly's steam yachts. In this picture, taken at Andover in 1968, it is in the ownership of Chris Edmonds of Princes Risborough.

A year or two later the Marenghi organ transferred to Lord Montague of Beaulieu, who owned it until 1999. He named the organ *Lady Hamilton*, which was very appropriate when it was posed alongside his Burrell showman's engine *Lord Nelson*.

Convertible roller No. 48946 *Ironside* is exhibited at Andover in 1968. The engine was built in 1924, one of the last under the Clayton & Shuttleworth name before the firm's purchase by Babcock & Wilcox. The ring of bolts around the smokebox flange facilitates its conversion to a conventional traction engine by replacing the front roll with ordinary road wheels.

Tasker tractor No. 1928 *Little Giant* was coincidentally built in 1928 and is seen here at the Andover rally in September 1969. The distinctive rectangular brass Tasker maker's plate shows up well on the side of the drive casing, and the chain drive mechanism is just visible behind the rear wheel.

Burrell gold medal tractor No. 3458 *Defiance* rests at Andover in 1969. For many years it carried the ownership lettering of Shipman & Barker of Hurst, Berkshire, as here. Built in 1913, it was originally used for haulage and is still with the Barker family. There are several nice showman's living vans in the background.

Marshall roller No. 89549, then known as *The Love Bug*, is posed at Andover in 1969. According to the rally programme this machine was built relatively recently in 1950, although other sources say 1944. Distinctive Marshall features include the domed front roll attachment and the cast rear wheels.

In a change of location, Fowler showman's road loco No. 15653 *Renown* is at a late 1960s Great Western Society operating day on the Cholsey to Wallingford branch line. Built in 1920, *Renown* and its sister *Repulse* were bought new by J. Murphy of Gateshead to power his Proud Peacocks scenic railway.

The Feast crane and cable rollers are seen on the rear of *Renown*, which, in conjunction with a derrick pole that fitted to the base of the crane, eased the handling of the heavy scenic railway cars. The railway locomotive is GWR 2-6-2 big prairie tank loco No. 6106, which had been privately preserved after withdrawal from service by British Railways.

At the Montague Motor Museum, Beaulieu, autumn 1969 Fair Organ Festival are Sally Beach's three-abreast gallopers. They are in front of Palace House, with Burrell showman's locos *Lord Lascelles* behind and *Lord Nelson* in the distance.

The 89-key Gaudin organ of Beach's gallopers can be glimpsed between the brightly painted horses. The gallopers were built in 1893 by Savages of King's Lynn; they and the organ eventually went to America, but not before they had starred in the film *Oh What a Lovely War!*

With the early evening sun streaking across, Burrell No. 3887 *Prince of Wales* gently rocks as it generates power in 1969. Its extension chimney is erected to improve the draught in the firebox and to carry the smoke upwards. A Scammell diesel tractor can be seen in the right background, together with several sacks of the all-important coal fuel.

Resplendent in 1969 at Beaulieu is Burrell scenic showman's engine No. 3886 *Lord Lascelles*. The engine was built in 1921 and supplied new to Harry Gray, working his scenic railway ride until 1939 when it was laid up. *Lord Lascelles* went to Hardwick's yard in 1951 and was renamed *Tulyar* after the Derby winner of 1952, being bought for preservation in the mid-1960s.

The Gaudin Brothers 65-key organ owned by C. Edmonds, named *Victory*, is belting out the tunes at the 1969 Beaulieu event as *The Iron Maiden* provides the power. The Cornish shield can be seen on the front of *Iron Maiden's* dynamo complete with its fifteen besants or pawnbroker's gold balls with underneath the Cornish motto 'One and All'.

An interesting picture in 1969 showing not just an organ and part of a model showman's engine but also the old Montague Motor Museum building with a car on display inside. The organ was built by Arthur Bursens of Hoboken, Antwerp, who made furniture for dance halls as well as organs to provide the music for them. He was still building organs in the late 1970s.

Also at Beaulieu in 1969 is Burrell showman's road loco No. 3443 *Lord Nelson* from the drive gear side. It is posed by the gatehouse with its extension chimney in place. Note the distinctive larger than usual belly water tank.

From the flywheel side we can see Lord Montague's Burrell showman's engine No. 3443 *Lord Nelson*. It is providing power for the Marenghi fairground organ *Lady Hamilton*, just visible on the left.

Burrell scenic showman's engine No. 3938 *Quo Vadis* is seen in a broadside view generating at Beaulieu in 1969. Behind the chimney is the bracket and additional exciter dynamo, the means by which the heavy electrical load entailed in starting a scenic railway ride was gradually ramped up.

A view of Edward Hine's Gavioli 89-key Black Forest Continental fair organ at Beaulieu in 1969. The instrument was built by Gavioli and restored by Carl Frei & Sohn of Waldkirch in the Black Forest. Mr Hine became owner of the organ in 1966.

A view of John Beach's gallopers with various showman's engines on the gravel drive outside Palace House at the Beaulieu Fair Organ Festival in 1969.

This Arburo 88-key dance organ *Rainbow,* built in 1928, is part of the Claude Jessett collection based at Tinker's Farm, Sussex. It is illuminated ready for an evening's music at Beaulieu and has a real saxophone, accordion and drum kit that actually play to accompany the organ music.

A time exposure of Burrell *Lord Nelson* all lit up and generating for the *Lady Hamilton* organ, ready for an evening entertaining the Fair Organ Festival visitors in 1969.

At Beaulieu around 1970, Burrell scenic showman's loco No. 3887 *Prince of Wales* is now seen in the ownership of L. J. Searle & Sons of Horsham. It is being admired by my father and generating for their Mortier & Gavioli organ *Matilda*.

Under restoration in around 1969 at the yard of J. Hirst, Hurstbourne station, Hampshire, is Wallis & Steevens roller No. 2656 *Little Olga*. It was originally built in 1903 as a tractor and converted into a roller during the 1920s. In recent years it has been reconverted back into a tractor.

A view of Hirst's Hurstbourne station yard with various steamrollers, all now cold and silent, most of which appear to be of Burrell manufacture.

A very large portable engine, believed to be Clayton & Shuttleworth No. 50004 built in 1926 and now restored and known as *Old Hiram*, sits in the yard. Some painted decoration remains on the flywheel. Portable engines needed to be towed from job to job, hence the towing bar fitted to the front axle.

Foden and Sentinel steam wagons, some of which appear to have originated in the former W. J. King of Taunton fleet, slowly rust away in the yard. I wonder if these, like the roller *Lorna Doone* in the next picture, have since been restored.

In the middle of the picture Burrell roller No. 4062 *Lorna Doone*, built in 1927, is seen awaiting its fate. The future would smile positively on *Lorna Doone*, but not as a roller, as it has since been converted into a steam tractor. The roller on the right is of Wallis & Steevens origin.

A close-up of the builder's and owner's plates of Burrell roller No. 4062 *Lorna Doone*. The owner's plate, above the nameplate, proclaims it to have come from the erstwhile W. J. King fleet based at Bishops Lydeard, Taunton. The brass builder's plate proudly proclaims: 'Chas. Burrell & Sons Limited, Manufacturers, Thetford, England, No 4062'.

Fowler roller No. 15902 *Jessica* of 1923 sits in the sun at the former Ashford Steam Centre, Kent, on the occasion of the visit by participants in the Southern Electric Group's 'Man of Kent' rail tour on 11 April 1971. Various Southern Railway steam locomotives were kept at Ashford until the site closed.

Following the decision to rebuild the Basingstoke town centre in the mid-1960s, Wallis & Steevens, builders of traction engines, road rollers and agricultural equipment, had to move from their North Hants Ironworks, Station Hill, Basingstoke, to the new Daneshill Industrial Estate where their Advance roller No. 7867, built in 1926, is on display.

This photograph of Simplicity roller No. 7940, built in 1928, was also taken at the Daneshill factory of Wallis & Steevens. The roller is now in the Milestones Museum, Basingstoke. These rollers were designed with a tilted boiler that ensured that the firebox and boiler tubes were always covered with water even when working on a slope.

The next few photographs are of the Historic Commercial Vehicle Club's annual London to Brighton run on 2 May 1971. Here is Sentinel DG4 four-wheeled wagon No. 8109 *The Chiltern Hundreds* approaching the end of its journey in the Old Steine, Brighton. It is mounted on cast wheels with solid rubber tyres.

Sentinel DG6 six-wheeled wagon No. 8213, built in 1930, is being overtaken in 1971 by a Guy Arab bus of the Provincial, Gosport & Fareham Company. The Sentinel wagon is on solid cast wheels and solid rubber tyres. The Sentinel's rear wheels are carried railway-style by an equalised bogie, which is chain-driven from the engine both to and within the bogie.

Sentinel DG6P six-wheeled wagon No. 8590 of 1931 is passing Brighton Aquarium and Dolphinarium as it proceeds along Madeira Drive. The 'P' designation indicates the wagon is fitted with pneumatic tyres. This wagon was originally preserved in 1962 and has since been rebuilt as a bus and named *Elizabeth*.

Parked on Madeira Drive, Brighton, is Foden steam wagon No. 13138 *London Pride*. This featured earlier at an Andover rally when in the ownership of Boughtons. Here it is owned by J. W. Hardwick of Ewell.

Two steam wagons are posed on Madeira Drive along with the famous 1936 Renault omnibus from Paris. On the left is Sentinel wagon No. 1286 built in 1916, one of the earliest of this make. The Brown Bailey Steelworks in Sheffield was still using steam wagons as late as 1970. Next to it is Yorkshire wagon No. 652 built in 1914, with its boiler mounted transversely across the chassis.

A general view of a fairground laid out on the local common like so many village fairs over the years. This is Hungerford Olde Tyme Fayre and Steam Engine Rally on 13 June 1971. From left to right are Stoke's 'Big Eli' Ferris wheel, the Coronation Speedway ark, Dormans gallopers, Harry Lee's steam yachts, a lighthouse slip or helter-skelter and Emmett's chair-o-planes.

Here at the same event we see Harry Lee's steam yachts, *Columbia* and *Shamrock*, named after the famous J Class America's Cup racing yachts. The ride was built by Savages of King's Lynn in 1900 and at this time was still owned by the same fairground family. The organ is a 46-key Chiappa instrument.

Fairground tradition is being upheld on Sunday 13 June 1971 as a religious service is conducted from the platform of Dorman & Sons three-abreast golden gallopers. These gallopers were built by Savages in 1887 and are steam-powered by centre engine *Dreadnought*, with an 89-key Gavioli organ providing the music.

This magnificent machine is the most reminiscent of a scenic railway ride that I have seen. The Coronation Speedway ark was built by Orton & Spooner for Harry Gray in 1937 to commemorate the coronation of George VI. It is restored to its original form, including the impressive extension frontage with its four carved and gilded atlante figures and Ben Hur chariot race decoration.

Also attending the Hungerford rally was Wallis & Steevens general-purpose traction engine No. 3555 *Pedler*, shown here belted up to an operational threshing machine.

At the Andover Steam & Vintage Rally in September 1971 we see the three-abreast gallopers of Jimmy Williams. The rounding boards are beautifully decorated with wild animal scenes.

In this view the 87-key Gavioli organ and steam centre engine *Patrina* are both visible between the horses. A couple of years later this magnificent machine left these shores when it was exported to America.

This is the well-known Fowler showman's road loco No. 20223 *Supreme*, built in 1934. Perhaps this was the magnificent engine's first outing in preservation as the 1971 Andover rally programme stated that the engine 'is not at work and is for exhibition only'.

Mounted in its 1960s Bedford lorry is the 89-key Limonaire fair organ of J. and M. Keeley. The organ was made in 1898 and is receiving close examination by three very young, and one not so young, admirers at the 1971 Andover rally.

Here at Andover in 1971 is Wallis & Steevens No. 7115 *Boxer's Beauty* again. This time it is without a canopy but harnessed to a very well-restored Ransomes threshing machine.

On the rally field at Andover in 1971 we have another view of the wonderful Fowler showman's engine No. 20223 *Supreme*, owned and restored by Jack Wharton.

In May 1972 I visited the Basingstoke Steam & Transport Festival and what more appropriate way to start than the Thornycroft No. 1 steam van built in 1895. This was made at their Chiswick works, but the firm later moved to Basingstoke where they became famous for their Mighty Antar haulage trucks.

An American ex-US Army Dodge 6×6 truck gives a helping hand to a Sentinel steam wagon. The Sentinel No. 5509 was built in 1924 and in 1929 was acquired by Westmore Ltd of Newport, Isle of Wight, in whose colours it is seen here. It was purchased for preservation in 1967.

A surprise visitor to the 1972 Basingstoke event was Fowler No. 15657 *The Iron Maiden*, seen here being admired by a couple of young families. Prior to starring in the film *The Iron Maiden* it was named *Kitchener*. There is a rather nice Hillman Imp car parked by the hedge on the right.

Later, quite a crowd gathered around to listen to Edward Hine's Black Forest Gavioli Continental fair organ, power for which is being generated by Fowler *The Iron Maiden*. The Noyce family's beautiful golden gallopers are visible in the background.

Fowler showman's road loco No. 15319 *Queen Mary* was built in 1919 as a haulage engine for the War Department. It was sold to Portland Stone Quarries, Dorset, in 1920. In 1929 it was acquired by Townsend Amusements of Weymouth, converted to a showman's engine and used by them until 1946.

The arena line-up of showman's engines on the Basingstoke rally field in 1972. From left to right they are Garrett No. 33545 *Pride of Surrey* and Fowlers *The Iron Maiden*, *Queen Mary* and *Renown*.

Fowler roller No. 15970 *Carole* is seen in the arena line-up at Basingstoke. It was purchased from a scrapyard for preservation in 1968. The roller is fitted with scarifying equipment attached to the rear axle.

On the left is Aveling light steam tractor No. 11486 *Anne Marie*, built in 1926 and designed to be operated by one person at up to 5 mph. Alongside is Ruston Proctor steam tractor No. 52453 *The Lincoln Imp*, built in 1918.

At another Beaulieu fair organ festival is Garrett showman's tractor No. 33545 *Pride of Surrey*, built in 1919 by Richard Garrett & Sons of Leiston, Suffolk. At this time, it was in the ownership of E. J. North.

Also at Beaulieu, McLaren showman's road loco No. 1623 *Goliath* is generating by the gallopers. This large and powerful engine was built in 1917 as a gun haulage engine for the War Department, later being sold to the well-known showman Pat Collins, who converted it to showman's specification.

Fowler showman's engine *The Iron Maiden* has historic Palace House, Beaulieu, as a backdrop while generating power for Lord Montague's Marenghi organ *Lady Hamilton*. Recordings are being sold to the right of the organ and I still have the EMI LP, which I purchased here.

In 1921 Burrell scenic showman's engine No. 3888, *General Gough*, was supplied new to Swales Bolesworth to accompany their Venetian gondola switchback ride. After being owned by another show family it ended up being rescued from a disused gravel pit and preserved as shown here in the ownership of Mr F. J. Miller.

Owned since it was new solely by the De Vey family, proprietors of the Anderton & Rowlands fair, this was the first time since his childhood that my father had seen their mighty Marenghi military band organ. It is still in its original organ truck, which would have been proudly placed in the centre of their wonderful Golden Dragons scenic railway ride.

A mammoth dance hall organ built by the firm of Remond Duwyn is seen playing at Beaulieu. This one appears to have had an accordion added in front of a rank of pipes, probably by the firm of Decap, which built jazz band and electronic organs.

In the shadow of Palace House, Beaulieu, Fowler showman's engine *Supreme* is being admired by the crowd as it generates power to light the gallopers.

Burrell scenic showman's engine No. 4000 *Ex Mayor* is positioned by the gatehouse at Beaulieu. Compared with my earlier picture where it was in Burrell maroon livery, here it is back in the more familiar blue colour scheme of amusement caterer G. T. Tuby.

The fairground organ *Victory*, built by Gaudin Brothers of Paris, is looking very colourful as it belts out the tunes at Beaulieu.

Here is a time exposure of Fowler *The Iron Maiden* all lit up for the evening at Beaulieu, with my father, Jimmy, leaning against the tender. It is almost impossible to portray traction engines pin-sharp in time exposures as they constantly rock, almost imperceptibly, to and fro.

The 20th Andover & District Model Engineering Society Steam and Vintage Rally was held in June 1972 at Longparish, Hampshire. On the field we see Foden general-purpose traction engine No. 9052 *Rob Roy* built in 1914. In the background is another engine and two Sentinel S4 steam wagons.

Foden general-purpose traction engine No. 9052 *Rob Roy* is engaged in a tug-of-war competition with men from the crowd. Middleton House, Longparish, forms a picturesque backdrop to the scene.

Not content to compete with just the men, an all-comer's tug-of-war was later waged by Ruston Proctor steam tractor No. 52453 *The Lincoln Imp*. For a moment or two it looked as though the crowd might have had the better of the engine, but not for long!

After its tug-of-war exertions, Ruston Proctor tractor *The Lincoln Imp* poses during a quiet moment with Fowler *Supreme* and Foden *Rob Roy* in the background.

The flywheel spokes are blurred as Wallis & Steevens traction engine No. 7115 *Boxer's Beauty* is seen again, belted up to a threshing machine. Notice the flywheel brake pad in front of the flywheel.

A close-up view of the cylinder and valve gear of *Boxer's Beauty*, showing well its builders' plate: 'Wallis & Steevens Ltd, Engineers, 7115, Basingstoke'. Notice the governor at top left, driven by belted pulleys from the crankshaft, which kept the engine turning over at a constant speed.

McLaren No. 1160 *The Favourite* looks very powerful from this low angle. Before starting work in Wiltshire, the engine won a gold medal at the 1912 Brussels Exhibition.

In the late afternoon sun, Burrell gold medal showman's tractor No. 3192 *St Bernard* is seen here from the gear side. It is in marvellous condition here at Longparish in 1972, and is still with the Gilbey family, which also owns Burrell scenic showman's engine *Perseverance II*.

Sentinel No. 5509 carries a three-way tipper body and was built in 1924. Seen here without the need for a tow, it sparkles in the late afternoon sunshine. Rather a nice clerestory-roofed showman's living van can be glimpsed behind.

Super Sentinel S4 No. 9163 was built in 1935. These wagons represented the last fling for road steam and were capable of being driven like a motor lorry, having a fair turn of speed up to 60 mph.

The next two pictures show two more of the superb Burrell gold medal tractors. This is No. 3626 *Jane Eyre*, built in 1914, seen standing outside the Cheddar Transport Museum in the early 1970s.

Burrell gold medal tractor No. 3191 *Furious* was built in 1910 and is seen here also in the early 1970s. I believe this picture may have been taken at Hollycombe. The engine has since been converted to showman's specification.

I need no excuse for showing Anderton & Rowland's Burrell showman's engine No. 3443 *Lord Nelson* again. The large Mather & Platt dynamo is being belted up, ready to do some generating. The dynamo belts were leather and there was a periodic slap sound as the riveted joint passed over the dynamo pulley.

Back on the rally field is Fowler showman's loco No. 15653 *Renown*, with its extension chimney in place. Despite the rain, it is drawing an admiring crowd.

Another visit to a Beaulieu Fair Organ Festival sees Edward Hine's superb Burrell scenic showman's engine No. 3938 *Quo Vadis* posed by the gatehouse while visitors admire another exhibit to the left.

Burrell showman's No. 2894 *Lord Fisher* was new in 1907 and is shown here generating alongside Beach's gallopers at Beaulieu. Originally it was named *Excelsior* by Stricklands Amusements, who travelled it with a bioscope show and subsequently a set of gallopers.

Burrell No. 2894, seen again at Beaulieu, was later acquired by Sally Beach, renamed *Lord Fisher*, as here, and after another change of ownership, *Centaur*. More recently it is known as *Pride of Worcester* and carries the inscription 'Stricklands Palace of Light' on its canopy boards.

The *Rodeo* spinning top switchback was presented in 1984 at the 16th Great Working of Steam Engines at Stourpaine Bushes. The *Rodeo* name was inspired by cowboy decoration on the base panels, although here they are in primer during redecoration by Vicki Postlethwaite. Irvin's 89-key Gavioli organ was on loan.

Perhaps the grandest organ of them all? The 98-key Gavioli organ was built in 1909 for the White Brother's *Electric Coliseum* bioscope show. It was later used in their Golden Dragon scenic railway ride until the late 1930s. By the 1950s it was in a bad state of repair and was moved north to Durham for preservation.

With its well-polished brasswork shining, Burrell No. 3890 *Majestic,* built in 1921, looks magnificent here at the 1984 Stourpaine Bushes event. It served with Herberts of Southampton from new until 1952.

The grand line-up of showman's engines with the old-time fair behind has been an iconic feature of the Stourpaine Bushes and latterly Great Dorset Steam Fair events for many years. This view shows a variety of showman's engines and tractors with plenty of smoke drifting across the sky.

The Iron Maiden is seen on a beautiful sunny day in 1984 with Harry Lee's steam yachts behind. Propped up against its front wheel is the cover for its dynamo switchgear, voltmeter and ammeter, which bears its original nameplate *Kitchener*, with which it was adorned in its pre-film star days.

Visitors are not always aware of the effort that goes into getting engines to and from a show and presenting them for several days. Here the owner or crew of Garrett showman's tractor No. 32122 *The Greyhound* is taking a well-earned break. The engine was built in 1918 and used by the Beach family.

Stourpaine Bushes and now the Great Dorset Steam Fair have always taken pride in presenting engines and tackle doing what they were designed for. Here is 1908-built Fowell general-purpose traction engine No. 97 *The Black Prince* and a threshing machine among bales of straw and haystacks. Just seven of the 101 Fowell engines survive that are known to have been made.

Marshall three-speed, fully sprung traction engine No. 57304 *Challenger* is at work at the 1984 Great Dorset Steam Fair with a threshing machine and, on the right, a baler. The engine was built in 1911 and is understood to be the only one of its type in preservation.

A small steam tractor built in 1902, Wallis & Steevens No. 2694 *Goliath* was owned by G. J. 'Doc' Romaines. Here it is paired up at the 1984 event with his 1944-built Ransomes, Simms & Jefferies threshing machine.

After all that hot work feeding the threshing machine, what better than a nice cooling drink of cider! Here is Foden wagon No. 13316 of 1929 *Sir Lionel*. This wagon worked as a tar tanker until the 1950s when it was bought for preservation.

At the top of the hill at Stourpaine Bushes is Fowler K7 ploughing engine No. 15517 *Hilary*, built in 1920. Ploughing engines work in pairs and it is most likely that the engine just visible at the bottom of the hill is its sister, No. 15516 *Ruth*. These two engines worked together on the Smith's Potato Crisps estate in Lincolnshire until 1949 and were bought for preservation in 1973.

The Fowler anti-balance plough, weighing around 6 tons and over 30 feet in length, has been winched from the bottom of the hill. The anti-balance design prevents the raised part from tending to lift the rear plough out of the ground. By contrast a modern tractor ploughs the field in the far distance.

This 1984 picture of Fowler No. 14256 *General French*, built in 1916, shows the drive train via gears, shafts and a clutch mechanism from the flywheel crankshaft to the cable drum beneath the boiler. The cable is fed through a pulley system that raises and lowers it smoothly onto the winding drum.

McLaren heavy haulage road locomotive No. 1652 *Boadicea* was built in 1919. Intended by the War Office to haul guns, it never served abroad. *Boadicea* was later purchased by a showman, converted to full showman's specification and renamed *Gigantic*. Too heavy for fairground work, it was sold into heavy haulage and was bought for preservation in 1958.

Burrell road locomotive No. 3057 *Lord Roberts* is winching some heavy concrete piping onto a solid-wheeled trailer using the cable wound round the winding drum on its nearside rear axle. On the right is a typical living van used by haulage, ploughing and threshing crews.

Having loaded the trailer, Burrell *Lord Roberts* is leading McLaren *Boadicea* with Burrell No. 3593 *Duke of Kent* bringing up the rear. These three were demonstrating haulage under the name 'Amalgamated Heavy Haulage'. In practice, single engines would manage much heavier loads such as boilers on their own, but this ensemble creates a memorable spectacle.

Two Burrell princesses are side by side. On the left is Burrell No. 3949 *Princess Mary*, built in 1923 for William Nichols of Forest Gate with a lower-arched canopy to negotiate low bridges in areas of London. It was part of the Hollycombe Fairground collection until 1982. On the right is Burrell No. 3847 *Princess Marina*, built in 1920, which spent most of its working life in East Anglia.

Fowler showman's road loco No. 14934 *Monarch of the Road* was built in 1917 and spent most of its life in agriculture. It was converted into a showman's engine by D. G. Corbin in whose ownership it is seen here. The engine has since moved to a museum in Germany.

This 1984 picture shows Burrell scenic showman's engine No. 3887 *Prince of Wales* with its crane and derrick pole set up. The cranes were used to move the heavy scenic railway cars between a road trailer and the ride. On the right is Fowler tractor No. 19050 *Princess Royal*, built in 1931 and rebuilt as a showman's tractor in the late 1970s.

Burrell scenic showman's engine No. 3912 *Dragon* has been rallying for many years. Built in 1921 for West of England showmen Anderton & Rowlands, it was heavily embellished with decorative brasswork. *Dragon* and its sister *Earl Beatty* were supplied with smaller rear wheels to ease travelling the hilly West Country routes without having to stop to change gear.

The next few pictures were taken in 1987 when the Stourpaine event took place at nearby Everley Hill. At the wood sawing bench is Marshall general-purpose engine No. 3633 *Hayden Princess*. It was built in 1901 and used for threshing and timber hauling. The general layout can be seen, with a baulk of timber being lined up with the circular saw blade in order to be sliced into planks.

An anti-balance plough is being hauled down the steep field at Everley Hill by an unidentified Fowler ploughing engine. One side of the plough would comprise left-handed blades and the other side right-handed blades, ensuring that as the plough was hauled to and fro all the furrows were turned over in the same direction.

A Fowler on the left and on the right a McLaren ploughing engine, No. 1552 *Hero*, are seen here. A cultivator, or large rake, is being hauled down the hill to break up the soil surface.

A real old timer is seen here, Fowler ploughing engine No. 1368 *Margaret*. Built in 1870, it is one of the oldest traction engines in existence, along with its sister *Noreen*, built in 1873. *Margaret* dates from the very earliest days of steam ploughing using the cable system between two engines.

A group of children take a break by the gallopers built by Savage's of King's Lynn in 1896.
They were supplied new to Harry Gray of Hampstead Heath but stood derelict from the 1940s.
The exotic wild animal paintings on the rounding boards were revealed during restoration
in the 1980s.

All the fun of the fair! Noyce's gallopers were also built by Savage's in 1895. Originally supplied
to the Studt family, they then passed to the West of England showman J. Cole before being
purchased by the Noyce family in the 1950s. The Swingler's Foster engine No. 14564 *Victoria* is
seen on the end of the showman's engine line-up.

This is Clayton & Shuttleworth showman's engine No. 48656 *Old England*. It was built in 1920 as a traction engine and has been converted from scrapyard condition into a showman's engine. It has since been converted for a second time into a road haulage locomotive.

Here is Len Crane's Fowler B6 super lion road loco and crane engine No. 17212 *Wolverhampton Wanderer*. The engine was built in 1929 and used to deliver boilers and other heavy loads all over the country. On the right is his 48 keyless Chiappa organ, adapted from a Gavioli of the 1890s.

Jack Wharton is taking a quiet moment to polish up his magnificent Fowler B6 super lion showman's engine *Supreme*, which positively glistens in the sunshine. The chrome plating is very evident in this photograph, being entirely original and ordered by the engine's first owner, Mrs A. Deakin, to make the engine as up to date as possible.

Another of the last four Fowler B6 super lion showman's engines, No. 19783 *King Carnival II* was built in 1932 for a Hartlepool showman who used it until 1941. It was then stripped of its showman's fittings and used for war haulage duties. It was preserved in 1968 and returned to full showman's specification.

At the 1987 Lingfield Park Racecourse rally we see another Burrell scenic showman, No. 3909 *Winston Churchill*, when in the ownership of J. W. Hardwick & Sons. It was supplied new to Hollands and named *Prince Albert* to power their Golden Dragon and Peacock scenic railway ride. In a derelict state it was bought direct from Hollands for preservation in the early 1950s.

Burrell showman's No. 3878 *Island Chief* is also seen here at Lingfield Park. It was built in 1921 for Alf Payne of Hull, who originally named it *Excelsior*. Arnolds of the Isle of Wight were its next owners, and named it *Island Chief*. In the late 1940s it was bought for agricultural work.

Burrell showman's engine No. 3894 *Saint Brannock* was built in 1921 as a haulage engine and converted to showman's specification in the 1920s. In the 1940s it was sold back into haulage and worked until the 1960s. Also here at Lingfield is a miniature general-purpose traction engine.

Commander Baldock established the fairground at Hollycombe and this 1989 view shows Burrell showman's engine No. 1876 *Emperor*. It was built in 1895 for Twigdons, who travelled the Midlands, and is unique in having an early open-framework dynamo. It served for some years as a crane engine. Behind *Emperor* are the steam gallopers, made by Tidman of Norwich around 1912.

At Hollycombe, *Dawn of the Century*, a bioscope show like those that brought the first movies to the public, can be experienced. A typical aspect of a bioscope show was music to attract the crowd, as provided here by the 98-key Marenghi Peacock organ, which plays popular music of the time.

The Garrett showman's tractor No. 33348 *Leiston Town*, built in 1918, provides the electric power to operate the lighting, organ, movie and magic lantern projectors in the bioscope show.

My father remembered seeing Burrell scenic showman's engine No. 3896 *Earl Beatty* at Redruth Fair during his childhood. At the 2005 Great Dorset Steam Fair *Earl Beatty* made its appearance following a long period of restoration. It is seen here with its extension chimney in place alongside the Anderton & Rowlands Grand Organ.

Among my father's recollections was the brightly polished brass bell, seen here attached to the side of the engine tender, and used to communicate between the operator of the Golden Dragons scenic railway ride and the *Earl Beatty* engine crew. Also shown on the Grand Organ truck is the unique original control panel, which controlled all electrical aspects of the ride.

The main dynamo and the exciter dynamo fitted to its special bracket between the chimney and cylinders of *Earl Beatty* are seen here together with much polished brass. The cylinder block and valve motion cover plates are decorated with brass stars and other brass trimmings, including nickel plated nuts. The swaged brass boiler bands are also visible.

Although sister engine *Dragon* was fitted with a tender crane extension bracket, it never carried the top crane pulley fitting seen here on *Earl Beatty*. The crane cable is carried on the winding drum mounted on the rear axle behind the nearside wheel and fed out through the nickel-plated rollers and painted pulleys to the top of the crane pole.

The magnificent Anderton & Rowlands Grand Organ is 'Playing the Melodies of the Masters' with power being provided by Burrell showman's engine No. 3159 *The Gladiator*. The engine was new to Anderton & Rowlands in 1909 to travel and light their Venetian gondola switchback ride. Sold to Whiteleggs in 1932, in 1953 *Gladiator* was bought for preservation by the Redruth Gladiator Club.

Anderton & Rowland's Burrells, *Gladiator*, *Earl Beatty* and *Dragon*, are pictured with the Grand Organ. What a splendid sight these engines would have made alongside the glittering Golden Dragons scenic railway, reputed to cost £40,000 new, including the 'twin' engines *Earl Beatty* and *Dragon*. Other rides were 'said to look commonplace and tawdry in comparison'.

Two Sentinels stand guard in 2005. In blue is Sentinel tractor No. 7527 built in 1928, while in maroon is Sentinel tractor No. 5644 *The Elephant* built in 1924. Now in Holland, *The Elephant* was delivered new to the Teignmouth Quay Company, Devon, and used to shunt railway wagons on the quay until preserved in the 1960s.

Parked at the top of the hill in blue livery is Marshall road loco No. 68632 *Ben Lomond,* built in 1915, and in front is Tasker B2 Little Giant convertible tractor No. 1513 *Twilight* built in 1912. Behind *Ben Lomond* is Garrett tractor No. 34789 *Cornish Star*, built in 1926, and at the very back is Burrell road locomotive No. 3824 *Lord Fisher of Lambeth*, built in 1919 and preserved in 1954.

Lots of smoke means the heavy haulage team is in action at the Great Dorset Steam Fair! Haulage engines are given a fairly free reign in the famous 'play pen' area as seen here. Fowler B6 crane engine No. 17106 *Duke of York* and McLaren *Boadicea* are pulling an articulated low-loader lorry and its Great Western Railway tank locomotive load up to the top of the hill.

While Burrell road loco No. 3057 *Lord Roberts*, with another traction engine for a load, pauses for a break, the two engines *Duke of York* and *Boadicea* are arriving at the top of the hill.

A contrast in heavy haulage. Fowler road loco No. 15323 *Excelsior* hauls a six-wheeled trailer loaded with a substantial log up the hill. *Excelsior* was built in 1918 for the War Department and was preserved in 1956. Behind it a Thornycroft Mighty Antar, built in 1961, is hauling a trailer with a military vehicle load. The Antar was delivered to the Royal Air Force for construction work.

Looking very smart at the 2005 Great Dorset Steam Fair and posed with a traction trailer and water cart is Marshall tractor No. 73900 *Jubilee* dating from 1920. The brass Marshall builder's plate is visible on the motion side cover.

Here is a close-up of the cylinder block and enclosed oil-bath valve motion on Wallis & Steevens tractor No. 7638 *Alice*, built in 1919. Behind is Robey steam tractor No. 41493 *Our Nipper* of 1924.

In the distinctive green livery it carried when working in Emerson and Hazard's ownership is Burrell showman's No. 3526 *Lightning II*. It was built in 1913 and preserved by the Prestons in 1957. It was reputed to be the only engine to leave the Burrell factory with green paintwork and is generating power for the Ruth organ alongside.

Seen here at the rather muddy 1987 Great Dorset Steam Fair in the showman's engine line-up is Fowler B5 No. 9177 *Dawn of the Century*. It was built in 1901 and worked until the 1920s when it was stored.

An unusual exhibit is Savage-built electric light engine No. 761. Like a portable agricultural engine, these had to be towed between fairgrounds. It was built in 1900 and used by Anderton & Rowlands to supply electric power to their bioscope show until the 1930s. It is the only one of its type left in the world.

Burrell showman's No. 3703 *Lady Mary* is seen here with its dynamo belted up, while the scorching on the lower smokebox would appear to indicate that it has been working hard. It was built in 1915 and the smooth brass cylinder side cover plate is unusual.

Some fairground atmosphere as the Noyce family's golden gallopers and Down's big wheel stop long enough for a time exposure. However, it is difficult to stop people moving, hence there are a few human 'ghosts' in the picture.

Another time exposure of the 1987 showman's engine line-up after dark, with Burrells *Lord Nelson* and *Princess Mary* nearest.

Burrell No. 3090 *Fermoy* all lit up after dark in the showman's line-up. It was new to Pool & Bosco in 1909. Alongside is Burrell *Princess Mary*.

The moon is casting a ghostly glow over the showground as quite a crowd ride on Noyce's gallopers. On the left is an 89-key Gavioli/Marenghi organ owned by showman J. Corrigan and later Tom Whitelegg.

A view of the spinning-top *Rodeo* switchback lit up for the evening. Compared with my earlier photograph, in this picture the side panels can be seen to have been decorated.

Burrell showman's road loco No. 3444 *His Lordship* was built in 1913. The engine spent years with the Green and the Silcock amusement concerns, being used until 1947. A couple of years later it was purchased for preservation.

En route to Cornwall in 2005 I attended a special open day at Dingles Steam Village in Devon, where outside the café was Burrell showman's road loco No. 3423 *Star*. It was supplied new in 1912 to T. Pettigrove, but by 1938 it was laid up and became in dire condition. In 1983 it was bought for preservation, restoration taking ten years.

Here is a showman's engine in its original workaday paintwork. Burrell No. 2804 *White Rose of York* was supplied to showman Alf Payne of York in 1906. In 1923, it was bought by Anderton & Rowlands. After some time with Heals of Glastonbury the engine moved to Pat Collins in the 1940s and was renamed *The Griffin*. It has been in preservation since the 1960s.

Foden steam wagon No. 13484 *Talisman* was built in 1930 as an estate tractor. As shown here, it is still mounted on cast wheels with solid rubber tyres.

Usually if you see traction engines on the road you don't have a camera with you! However, here is Allchin traction engine No. 3251 *Royal Chester*, built in 1925, which became the prototype for the well-known 'Matchbox Yesteryear' model. It is negotiating a roundabout at Winchester Road, Basingstoke, and in the background is a Bristol Lodekka bus on a local service.

Here at the 2004 Great Dorset Steam Fair is an agricultural scene with, in the foreground, a cultivator about to be hauled back across the field, and two ploughing engines behind.

Ransomes Simms & Jefferies portable engine No. 43030 *Harvest Time*, built in 1921, is driving a Ransomes Simms & Jefferies threshing machine and stationary baler. It is believed the engine was sold by Ransomes as late as 1935. Portable engines are not self-powered and have to be towed between jobs.

Another Ransomes threshing machine is powered by Wallis & Steevens general-purpose engine No. 2694 *Goliath* built in 1903. Judging by the stack on the left they have a lot of work to get through! The engine is believed to be the only one to have attended all of the fifty Stourpaine Bushes and Great Dorset Steam Fairs.

In the play pen at the 2004 Great Dorset Steam Fair an Aveling & Porter roller, No. 8489, built in 1915, is pictured towing a Wallis & Steevens tar spreader. In the far background two showman's engines can be seen, probably Burrells *Quo Vadis* and *Earl Beatty*, which had been delivered to the site earlier.

This picture shows Burrell road loco No. 3257 *Clinker* in the 2004 Great Dorset Steam Fair play pen with a trailer and traction engine load. *Clinker* was built in 1911 and used in haulage for many years before being used in the fenland area for dredging.

Late in the afternoon the setting sun catches the rounding boards of Down's gallopers. The gallopers were made by Tidman of Norwich and on special occasions such as this are still steam-powered by *John Bull*, a Savage centre engine.

Two of the Fowler B6 super lion showman's road locos are seen side by side in the 2004 showman's engine line-up, both wearing their first owners' names on their canopy side boards. On the left is *Supreme* and on the right is No. 19782 *Lion*. The latter engine was built in 1932, being supplied new to Anderton & Rowland, and recently changed hands for over £900,000.

Fowler super lion showman's engine *Lion* receives a polish from a junior member of the crew. The owner's plate, reading 'Anderton & Rowlands, Amusement Caterers, Bristol', can be seen on the toolbox above the belly tank.

The nameplate of *Lion* is pictured here with the owner's details – 'Anderton & Rowland Amusement Caterers' – on the dynamo support bracket. The screw adjuster handle hanging vertically is used to move the dynamo backwards or forwards to correctly tension the dynamo drive belt.

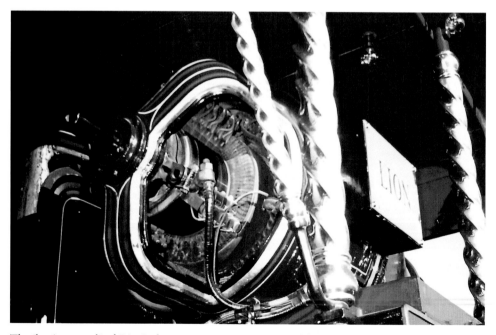

The 'business end' of *Lion*'s dynamo armature is captured here while generating. Three of the four sets of five-in-line commutator brushes are visible while the commutator segments have become a blur as the electrical power is pumped out.

The characteristic dished flywheel of Fowler *Lion* is shown to good effect in this picture together with the brass decoration and intricate detail of the multicoloured paint and gold leaf lining.

By contrast the flat face of the flywheel on this and most other showman's engines is shown in this 2004 picture of Aveling & Porter No. 6091 *Duchess*, built in 1906 and converted into a showman's engine.

Catching the late afternoon sun in front of the showman's engine line-up is Burrell special scenic showman's engine No. 3888 *General Gough*. The sunlight brings out the lovely rich maroon livery carried by this engine. Behind the chimney the bracket carrying the exciter dynamo can be seen, which facilitated enhanced electrical control of the heavy scenic railway rides.

To end with, as the evening sun sets after a nostalgic day it highlights the twisted brass canopy supports and extension chimneys of the engines in the showman's engine line-up at the 2004 Great Dorset Steam Fair.